I'm Longer Than You!

An Epic Contest of Measurement

For Kieran. Okay, I admit it, YOU are taller than ME!

Acknowledgments

A big thank you to Dr. Scott Persons, paleontologist at the College of Charleston, and to Dr. John Ryan, biological oceanographer at the Monterey Bay Aquarium Research Institute, who were kind enough to take a look at this manuscript. (Any mistakes are mine, not theirs.)

Text and Illustrations © 2025 Carolyn Fisher

All rights reserved. No part of this publication may be reproduced, stored in a retrieval system or transmitted, in any form or by any means, without the prior written permission of Kids Can Press Ltd. or, in case of photocopying or other reprographic copying, a license from The Canadian Copyright Licensing Agency (Access Copyright). For an Access Copyright license, visit www.accesscopyright.ca or call toll free to 1-800-893-5777.

Published in Canada and the U.S. by Kids Can Press Ltd.
25 Dockside Drive, Toronto, ON M5A 0B5

Kids Can Press is a Corus Entertainment Inc. company

www.kidscanpress.com

The illustrations in this book were created by hand by a human artist, Carolyn Fisher, who drew them with a stylus on a tablet.
The text is set in Playtime With Hot Toddies.

Edited by Katie Scott
Designed by Mike Reis

Printed and bound in Shenzhen, China, in 3/2025 by C & C Offset

CM 25 0 9 8 7 6 5 4 3 2 1

Library and Archives Canada Cataloguing in Publication

Title: I'm longer than you! : an epic contest of measurement / by Carolyn Fisher.
Names: Fisher, Carolyn, 1968– author, illustrator
Identifiers: Canadiana (print) 20240518853 | Canadiana (ebook) 20240518896 | ISBN 9781525312946 (hardcover) | ISBN 9781525313073 (EPUB)
Subjects: LCSH: Units of measurement — Juvenile literature. | LCSH: Weights and measures — Juvenile literature. | LCSH: Body size — Juvenile literature.
Classification: LCC QC90.6 .F57 2025 | DDC j530.8/1—dc23

Kids Can Press gratefully acknowledges that the land on which our office is located is the traditional territory of many nations, including the Mississaugas of the Credit, the Anishnabeg, the Chippewa, the Haudenosaunee and the Wendat Peoples, and is now home to many diverse First Nations, Inuit and Métis Peoples.

We thank the Government of Ontario, through Ontario Creates and the Ontario Arts Council; the Canada Council for the Arts; and the Government of Canada, for their financial support of our publishing activity.

I'M LONGER THAN YOU!

An Epic Contest of Measurement

Carolyn Fisher

KIDS CAN PRESS

OH YEAH? I'm as long as I'm as long as I'm as long as 21 fridges! I'm as long as 10 starfish! Well, I'm as long Big deal! Hey, shorty. Ha!

3 school buses!

I'm as long as a 10-story building!

I'm longer than an airplane!

I'm longer than 21 hockey sticks!

as a tall oak tree!

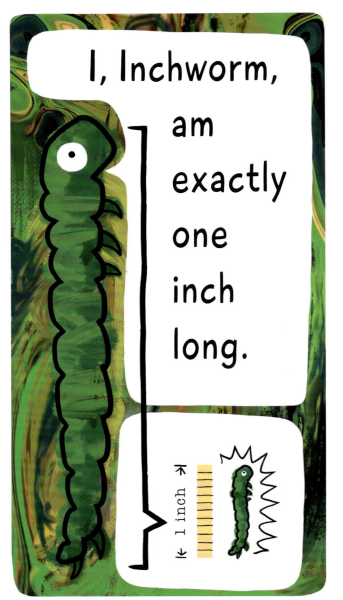

The loser will treat the winner to

LUNCH!

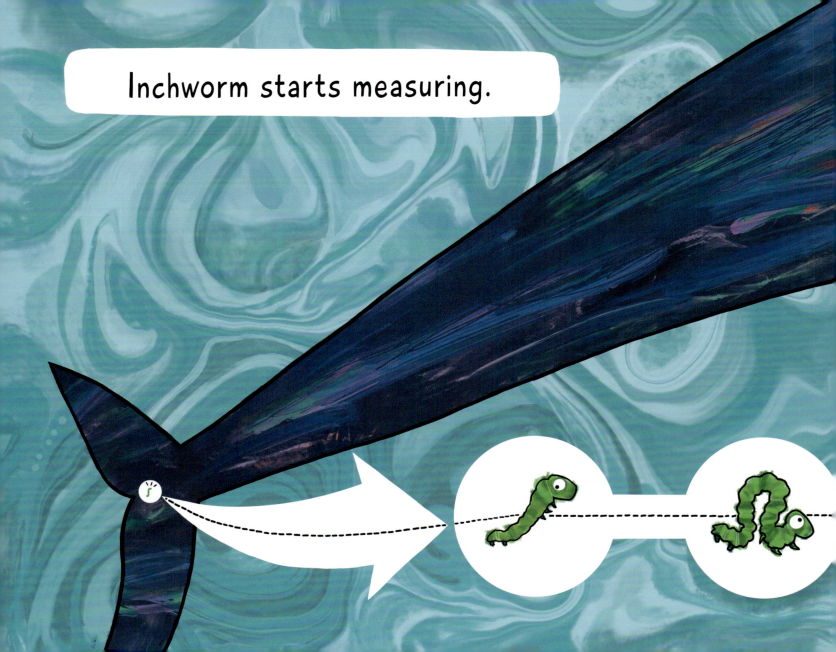

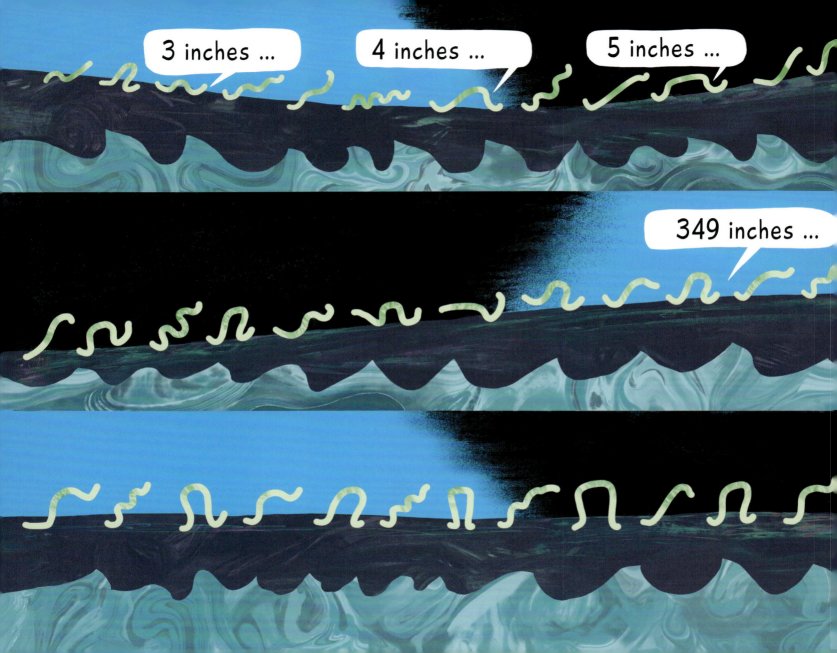

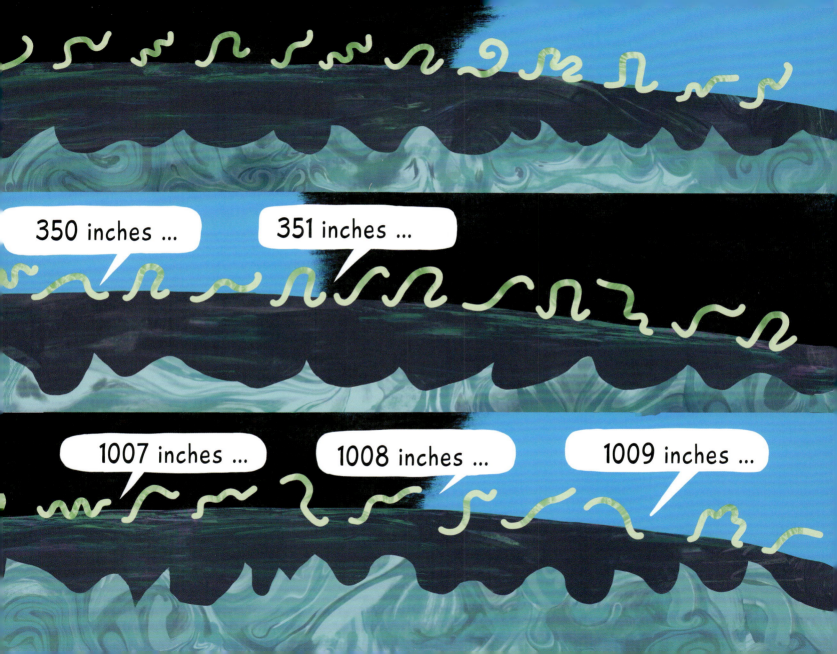

12 HOURS LATER

I have finished measuring Blue Whale ...

in inches!

I have good news ...

and bad news.

Blue Whale and I are having a contest to see who is longer.

The loser will treat the winner to lunch.

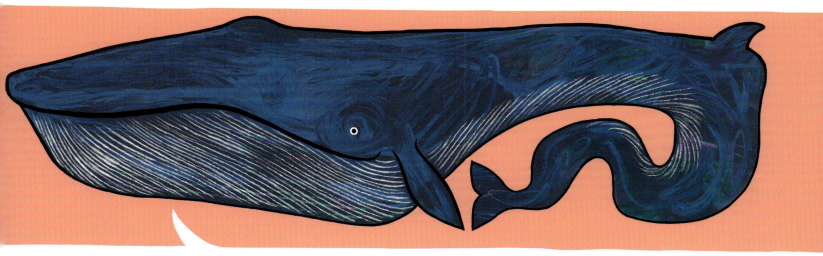

I, Blue Whale, am 1300 inches long.
But now we need to measure Supersaurus.

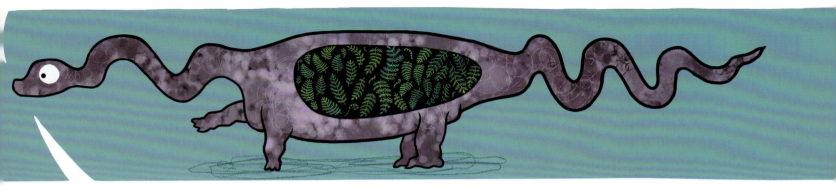

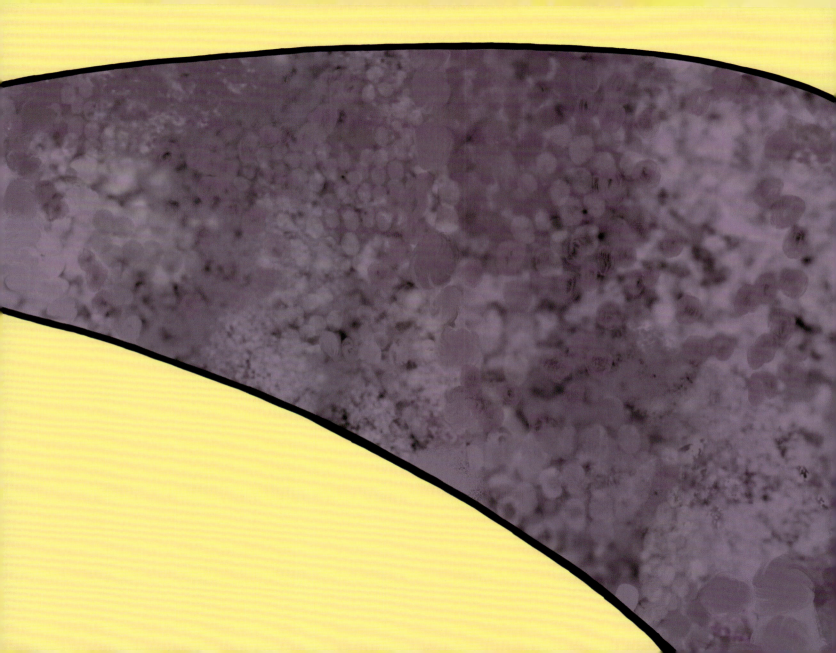

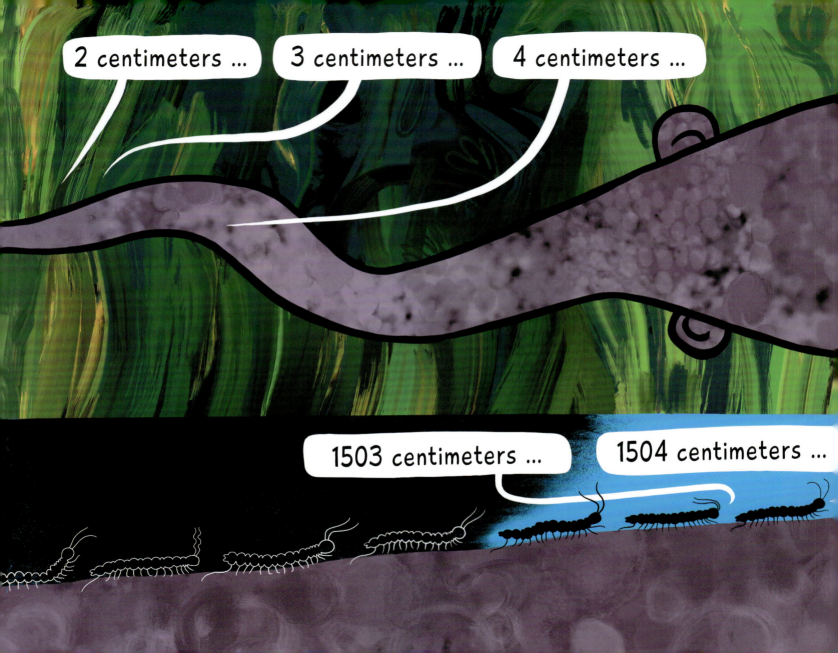

12 HOURS LATER
I, Centipede, have finished measuring Supersaurus ...
in centimeters.
I have good news ...
and bad news.

You can change inches to centimeters

WITH MATH!

Multiply the inches by 2.54 to get the number of centimeters!*

*Or divide the centimeters by 2.54 to get the number of inches!

3302 centimeters long!

> I had to count on ALL of my legs to do the calculation!

Meet the Cast

INCHWORM

Larva of peppered moth
(*Biston betularia*)

1 inch/2.54 centimeters

The inchworm gets its name for the way it crawls, as if inching along.

SUPERSAURUS

(*Supersaurus vivianae*)

1300 inches/3302 centimeters

CENTIPEDE

Stone centipede (*Lithobius microps*)

0.39 inches/1 centimeter

The word *centipede* means "hundred feet," but most centipedes have fewer than one hundred feet.

BLUE WHALE

(*Balaenoptera musculus*)

1300 inches/3302 centimeters

of the Story

Supersaurus belonged to a group of sauropod dinosaurs that lived about 145 million years ago. These long-necked creatures were enormous! Paleontologists have estimated the length of supersaurus from incomplete fossil skeletons. So if new supersaurus fossils are unearthed, then the length estimate of supersaurus might change.

DRAGONFLY
Giant darner (*Anax walsinghami*)
4-inch/10.16-centimeter wingspan

KRILL
North Pacific krill (*Euphausia pacifica*)
0.60 inches/1.52 centimeters

FERN
Cinnamon fern (*Osmundastrum cinnamomeum*)
72 inches/182.88 centimeters

Blue whales did not exist during the age of the dinosaurs. Blue whales came onto the scene about 1.5 million years ago, once Supersaurus had already been extinct for about 143.5 million years. So blue whales and dinosaurs never lived on Earth at the same time ... except in the author's imagination, and in this book!

PEOPLE HAVE INVENTED DIFFERENT WAYS OF MEASURING

In this book, Inchworm measures length in inches using the customary system. Centipede measures length in centimeters using the metric system. Some countries use the customary system, while other countries use the metric system. And some countries use a combination of both systems.

	LENGTH *How long?*	MASS *How heavy?*	VOLUME *How much?*	TEMPERATURE *How hot or cold?*
CUSTOMARY SYSTEM 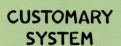	12 inches = 1 foot 3 feet = 1 yard 1760 yards = 1 mile	16 ounces = 1 pound 2000 pounds = 1 ton	8 fluid ounces = 1 cup 2 cups = 1 pint 2 pints = 1 quart 4 quarts = 1 gallon	water freezes at 32 degrees Fahrenheit water boils at 212 degrees Fahrenheit

METRIC SYSTEM	10 millimeters = 1 centimeter 100 centimeters = 1 meter 1000 meters = 1 kilometer	1000 milligrams = 1 gram 1000 grams = 1 kilogram 1000 kilograms = 1 tonne	1000 milliliters = 1 liter	water freezes at 0 degrees Celsius water boils at 100 degrees Celsius

METRIC PREFIXES

TERA	×	1 000 000 000 000 (one trillion)
GIGA	×	1 000 000 000 (one billion)
MEGA	×	1 000 000 (one million)
KILO	×	1000 (one thousand)

HECTO	×	100
DECA	×	10
DECI	÷	10
CENTI	÷	100

MILLI	÷	1000
NANO	÷	1 000 000 000 (one billion)

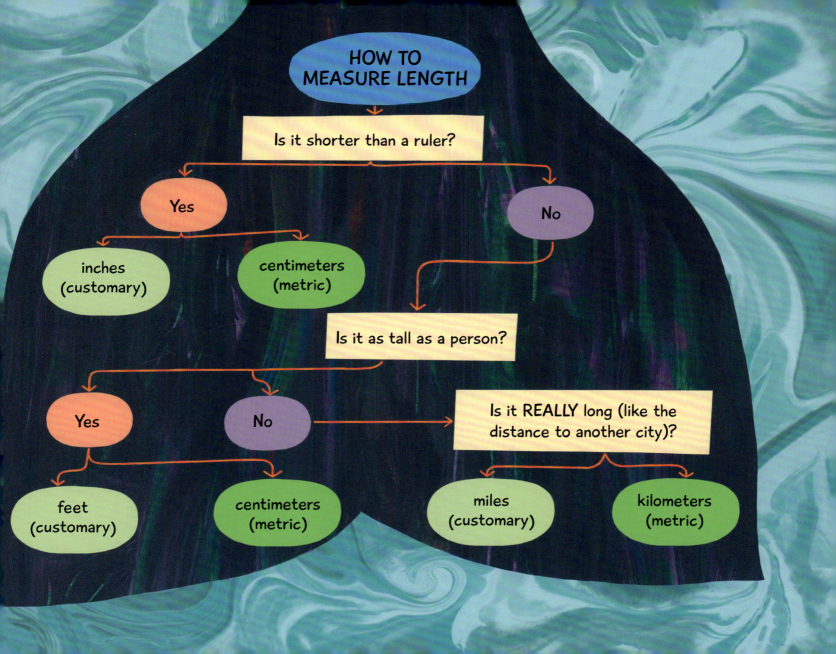

LIGHT-YEAR

Used to measure long distances, such as between planets. One light-year is the distance that light travels in one year, about 9.46 trillion kilometers or 5.88 trillion miles.

ZEPTOSECOND

The smallest unit of time, it's measured as a trillionth of a billionth of a second (or, 0.000000000000000000001 seconds).

SOME NON-STANDARD MEASUREMENTS

DONKEYPOWER

Engines are measured in horsepower (about 746 watts). Weak engines are measured in donkeypower — just divide the horsepower by three.

BARLEYCORN

An ancient unit of length, as long as a grain of barley.